Overcoming Racism

I0411969

The Ultimate Guide for How to Overcome Racism Forever

as so. The presentation of the information is without contract or any type of guarantee assurance.

The trademarks that are used are without any consent, and the publication of the trademark is without permission or backing by the trademark owner. All trademarks and brands within this book are for clarifying purposes only and are the owned by the owners themselves, not affiliated with this document.

Table Of Contents

Introduction

The pages in this short, concise book were developed through years of experiences that I have gone through, as well as what has proven to work for others that I have talked to and have researched.

After experiencing many different types of racism throughout my life and struggling to overcome these negative situations, I decided that I wanted to write a short, detailed book to help other people who are in a similar situation as I was. I also want to help people understand how racism forms and why people experience it, because there are many people who may have relatives or friends who are racist and are unable to relate to them without frustration.

You will find this book useful if you make sure to implement what you learn in the following pages. The important thing is that you IMPLEMENT what you learn. Racism is not conquered over night but the important thing to remember is that it is definitely possible for you to make a change.

Every person has unique experiences in their life that develop their worldview. Sometimes people realize later on in their life that they carry some negative beliefs around with them about people of different cultures or races. As you go through these pages, you'll get a better understanding of what racism really is, where it comes from, and you will learn several ways that you can overcome it.

We will dive into how your early childhood can influence the way you look at others, how society is affected by racism and racist ideas, methods on how to eliminate racism at home, school and at work, and why ensuring a racist-free society is the only way to make it better and productive.

It is recommended that you take notes while you are reading this book. This will ensure that you get the most out of the information in here. The notes will help you to pinpoint exactly what you need to take from the book, and by writing things down, you will be able to recall specifics and how to handle certain situations when they arise.

Lastly, remember that everything in this book has been compiled through research, my own experiences, as well as the experiences of others, so feel free to question what you have read in this book. It is encouraged that you to do your own research on the topics that you want to look deeper into. The more you understand regarding your own mind and body and those of the people around you, the better off you'll be. So remember to read with confidence and an open mind!

*While various forms of racism, colonialism, and slavery have occurred throughout the world in cultures of all forms, this book will use examples from the Western World, specifically the United States, to relate to readers. This is not meant to single out any specific country, color of people, religion, or ideology, etc. These are just examples!

Chapter 1:

Origins of Racism

In the last few years, racism has been one of the issues that managed to arrive at the forefront of mainstream media, thanks to mass movements such as Black Lives Matter and global political and economic issues, such as some nations refusing refugees from war-stricken countries, and news of discrimination against immigrants during the British exit from the European Union. With the increasing violence against people of different races, it is high time that racism is brought back into the spotlight, once again.

This is probably not the first writing that you will encounter about racism. While there is much tolerance towards people of differing origins, racism still exists in different forms.

If you know someone that has been refused of a basic human right such as access to employment, public transportation, or even citizenship, you must have realized that racism, as a concept, is capable of so much destruction -

to the point that people throughout the world face a devaluing of their own identity, and go as far as indiscriminate destruction of communities – something that nations that believe in democracy and the existence of human liberty and rights should not uphold.

Racism is defined in many dictionaries as a form of marginalization of people by basis of race, cultural backgrounds, nationalities, and even physical features. It is the belief that human characteristics, traits, and qualities are affected by race and nationality. It divides humanity into separate groups and labels others as either inferior or superior, and supports the idea that each race or nationality must be treated differently.

There are many scholars that disagree whether the term "racism" is inherently bad and suggests a negative meaning. This is the reason why most use the term "racial discrimination" to describe social injustices suffered by prejudices towards a particular "race" due to social, cultural, and physical differences. However, to know how to eliminate racism, one must first know what racism really entails, its history, and how racism developed in human society.

Defining Racism

One of the barriers that people face in overcoming racism and achieving real diversity is how they arrive at the definition of racism. Some people only reserve this term for black or white American bias, but in reality, racism is a global phenomenon that exists out of different economic, social, and political factors.

Because it can exist in different contexts and forms, it has been defined by Australia's Human Rights and Equal Opportunity Commission in 1998 as an ideology that provides expression to myths about different ethnic groups or races that rise from deeply-rooted cultural, social, historical, and power inequalities that exist within society.

Racism, as a concept, is a by-product of different interplays of institutional, individual, and social practices. You, as an individual, feel its effect when you encounter individual and institutional actions in ideologies that you experience in the mainstream context.

You may also encounter it in different forms, as social climate changes. For example, during the alleged manslaughter of black Americans in the hands of white American police and the height of the popularity of Black Lives Matter, there are movements that exist that attempt to downplay these crimes with the introduction of a counter movement called "All Lives Matter".

Another example is that during the announcement of Britain's exit from the European Union, news broke out that there were British citizens that called out for the quick exit of immigrants or anyone that appeared to belong to another race, without a thought about if the people that they wanted to remove from the country was a naturalized citizen or not.

Racism is also found influential in performing many social behaviors and traditions such as otherness, segregation, xenophobia, supremacism, and perceived hierarchical ranking in society. When these social phenomena happen, the ill effects of racism can be felt.

As the United Nations Declaration of Human Rights says, one can only treat others with dignity if he allows others to enjoy economic, social, political, and cultural rights, without having to qualify the status, sex, color, social origin, language, religion, or political opinion. When all of these factors are met, that is the only time that one allows others to truly enjoy civil liberty.

Within the same vein, the United Nations define racial discrimination as any act that restricts, assigns preference, excludes, or distinguishes people that do not share the same ethnic origin, color, or nationality.

Racial discrimination also occurs when the act of differentiating people holds the purpose of damaging or removing recognition of one's identity, the ability to enjoy or practice human rights, and the most fundamental human freedoms.

Academics and the Concept of Racism

In the past, the term "race" has been used to identify people that have different national or ethnic origins, to the point that taxonomy of individuals exist. Because people of different origins were previously classified in such a way that there are some races that are genetically favorable above others, different fields of science also contributed to the promulgation of racial hierarchy in the past.

Today, most sociologists, anthropologists, and biologists reject the idea that people from different ethnic origins come from different species that are inferior to the politically and socially dominant ones. In fact, some sociologists even make the claim that the idea of race is just a social construct, which means that it only exists within the social and individual realms – this means that any conclusions made about different races are heavily influenced by deep cultural ideologies.

According to W.E.B. Du Bois, racism is born out of beliefs that are culturally sanctioned, which means that because there are beliefs and assumptions that were long held by members of society, there are actions that are done against perceived racial minorities, with the attempt to defend these beliefs. It is also worth taking note that this defense of social norms happen outside of any intention – it is simply difficult to go against those belief systems, which have grown sturdy roots in society.

Racism Today

Because of the changing views about who should enjoy civil liberty and fundamental human rights, racism has also begun to change its form, thanks to progressive movements that have enabled different nations to change how racism should be viewed.

While racism has earned a negative sanction in society today, it is quite easy to say that it never disappeared but turned into a more covert form of prejudice. Since being overly discriminate against a minority group is fast becoming taboo, racism is not as explicit as it was in the past. However, since it has taken a different form that is harder to detect, it is now easy to blur the lines between racism and an innocent public opinion.

For this reason, ending racism becomes extra challenging since some people do not recognize that their actions already constitute aversion or hostility towards people that belong to another group. That means that in order to help end racism, one must be able to recognize personal actions that actually constitute discrimination towards others. That also means that people should understand why they have a hostile opinion towards others that behave or look differently.

If you think that you are capable of discriminating others because they have a different culture or ethnic origin, then it may be best to also understand where that behavior is coming from. It also helps to understand that racism happens because a dominant group enjoys benefits out of the discrimination or oppression of others, whether or not they express desire for such benefits.

Your experience of racism is also not limited to you being the one that is discriminated or not. Even if you are enjoying the rights of the dominating class or race, you may find that you are also suffering the consequences of racism through insecurity, misconceptions about people who should deserve privilege, and general negative attitude towards people that do not belong to the same racial class that you are a part of.

While there are people that seem to be away from the more violent conflicts involving racism, this ideology promotes a behavior that no one can be safe from – those that embrace discrimination against other races proliferate the thinking that they are unsafe around people who do not think, look, or act like them, while those that are objects of discrimination face the thought of violence against them. With this ideology around, no one feels safe wherever they are.

Racial Discrimination in History

The practice of racial discrimination was present in human society as far back as we have records for. As primitive man began to organize small communities, the natural instinct to be biased to one's own group was inherent. As communities grew and expanded, cultural differences continued to increase and the concept of "race" began to emerge.

It becomes quite easy to determine how people have learned to set boundaries around them and also adopt an ideology that will make them feel better than the rest of the world. Even the world's most important political philosophers have implanted a seemingly logical argument that inspired generation after generations of people thinking that class superiority exists.

For example, the philosopher and political scientist John Locke has made it a point that it is quite natural for human beings to have exclusive use for a particular resource. Friedrich Nietsche, on the other hand, developed the idea of the "superman", which argues that there are some races that are intrinsically weaker than others.

Even before the popularity of philosophical discourse favoring racial privilege, racial discrimination already existed. During the Greek and Roman times, the word "barbarian" became their term to call any culture that rejected Roman or Greek influences. For the Greeks, Persia was considered a nest of heathens, unruly people and a savage "race". A countless number of racist propaganda, from classical Greek authors, were indoctrinated to the Greek citizens telling them of the "brutality" of Persian barbarians.

This continued on with the Romans, as they waged war with Carthage and the inhabitants of Gaul and Germania. All of these cultures were considered "barbarian" by Roman standards, that should be subjugated, ruled on and enslaved, if necessary. During these ancient times, racial discrimination was focused on cultural differences.

Ancient civilizations have also established a deep institutional racism against people that have been conquered through expansion of empires – as an empire progresses and captures lands, all members of the communities that fell to military conquests are immediately seen as lower class citizens with limited to no rights at all.

Because of different beliefs and traditions held by these different cultures, it is easy for people belonging to the more powerful countries to devise myths that would make it reasonable for them to capture and "civilize" a community that has less military or economic power.

Over the previous centuries, the impact of Western discrimination against the less powerful civilizations and dynasties proved to have lasting effects, as it gave birth to the concept of "white supremacy". As European countries emerged, stemming from the Greek and Roman civilizations, continents that had thriving cultures are conquered as part of economic expansions from more powerful empires.

Since there is no better way to conquer a land than to remove the identity of its inhabitants, ancient conquerors have made it possible to instill the idea that conquered communities do not deserve any right at all by planting ideologies that make violence and discrimination against them seem reasonable.

Role of Religion in Racism

Religion played a vital role in the development of culture in every country. However, as religion has contributed to the creation of positive and family values, it has also led to another form of racism, which is religious discrimination.

However, it is also rather easy to say that religious discrimination could have easily risen from the political and economic power held by the more powerful countries that were discovering lands for their expansion during the rise of the ancient civilizations.

For example, the Arabs had practiced racism before they embraced Islam as one of their central religions. The early Egyptians established a system that promoted monarchy and societal hierarchy with the belief that this order in society was dictated by the gods.

However, one of the most far-reaching religious powers that has promoted deep racial bias is the Holy Catholic Church, dating back to the rise of the Holy Roman Empire, which conquered different territories in Europe and the Middle East. Tracing back the roots of the Catholic Church and its rise as one of the most far-reaching religions in the world today, the faith served as one of the most important tools of imperialism during medieval times.

During the middle ages, Catholicism was a major religious force in Europe. Almost 90% of the people in Europe were under the Catholic faith. As a consequence, all religious observance which was not in line with Catholic doctrine was considered pagan and immediately repressed.

It is also important to take note that the most powerful Western nations are given sanction by the Holy Catholic Church to expand their reach to undiscovered lands to promulgate Christianity. Since the Pope serves as a source of political and economic power for most Christian countries, setting sail to un-Christianized lands and converting non-believers became a part of every expedition.

In effect, the seemingly virtuous task of spreading the Gospel turned into a mask hiding oppression and persecution of non-Christians when powerful countries colonized new territories in the East and the "New World".

This feeling of religious superiority and the need to defend it from "pagan" influences was also the case with other major religions on Earth, namely Judaism and Islam. Being treated unjustly because of religious differences became a serious problem, which in some instances has continued until today.

While you may think that racism due to "backward" religious practices during the prevalence of strong religions such as Protestant and Catholic churches are gone with the times, sociologists were still able to discover that the racist behavior that can be experienced today and the religious leanings of people are still inter-related.

A study conducted by Michael Emerson showed a conclusion that less than 10% of the total United States congregations have about 20% population that are made up of people from a racial minority. In the United States, only 5% of the existing Protestant churches are found to be multi-racial. The United States Catholic churches, on the other hand, have only 15% of their congregations to be accepting members from a different race.

Perhaps among the reasons why some religious orders seem to support racist ideology is that some passages in the holy books, such as the Old Testament in the Bible, are interpreted to be supportive of racist practices.

For example, there is a passage in Deuteronomy that encourages Israelites to "smite and utterly destroy members of other ethnic groups that they will find inhabiting the Promised Land". While passages like these can be read in another light, there are practitioners that may take these parts of the Holy Bible literally and take belief that violence against others is sanctioned by God.

For this reason, there are different members of other Christian sects that feel that there are certain parts of the Holy Bible that offer conflicting statements against oppressive ancient practices such as racial discrimination and slavery – while there is a growing movement that encourages Christians to embrace the more empathic books included in the Bible, which promote unconditional love for everyone.

Racism in the United States

Racist sentiments in the United States started when the first English settlers managed to create communities in New England. These settlers began to take possession of the land and started to utilize it to their advantage. As English settlers expanded their territories, they began to establish contact with Native Americans which, in many instances, ended in conflict.

During the early part of the 18th century, the French-Indian wars ravaged the American colonies. This conflict with Native Americans started a racial stigma that affected English settlers in the years after. The savage "Indian" whose goal was to inflict harm to harmless settlers began to circulate in the colonies, which created discrimination towards Native Americans.

The image of savagery was gradually associated with the physical features of the Native Americans, which increased the level of racism within the new version of America.

In Summary

According to many sociology experts, the origins of racism are the cultural differences of communities, misunderstanding of their customs, religions, and conflict. To these experts, these factors are what has fueled the fire of racism in countries like the United States and in other parts of the Western World.

However, understanding how racism has been ingrained in influential countries like the United States will lead you to seeing that racism is essentially a social construct – by embracing a particular reading of another person's culture and behavior and sticking to the belief that a different set of attitudes is potentially harmful to the status quo, some societies have learned to think that oppression against minorities is an acceptable practice. On the other hand, it is also important to understand that these beliefs can be changed and updated.

It is important to remember that slavery and racial/religious discrimination has occurred in many different cultures and in many different eras throughout human history. This is one reason that some people are so frustrated that there are still so many acts of discrimination regarding equal rights when it comes to race, sexuality, and/or religious preference. In essence, they believe that we should have moved past this type of thinking already.

Chapter 2:

The Slavery-Racist Connection

Right after the Civil War, John L. Dawson stated that the prejudice that exists against other races exists for wise purposes. Within the same vein, Senator James Doolittle made a claim that racial discrimination is an instinct that exists within human nature and that men are compelled to sort others according to categories, and then ultimately falling to the fact that white people do have supremacy over other races.

With the claim that racism is, in fact, a natural human behavior, then there is that challenge when it comes to eradicating this globally widespread form of oppression. On the other hand, there is also this argument that within the heart of this oppression is that certain societal processes created racism as people know it now.

Karl Marx, in his work *Wage Labor and Capital*, states that men of the black race become slaves because of certain societal relations that are perpetuated by capitalism, or simply put - human greed.

When we look at the privileged and the supposed supremacy of other races, then we can easily see that certain practices, such as slavery, exist because races with economic and religious power can easily draw the line between themselves and the people that they want to colonize. As historian Eric Williams put it, slavery and other oppressive capitalist practices was technically not born out of racism, but the other way around.

When talking about racism, one cannot discount the fact that alongside racism is the shadow of slavery. The connection with slavery and how racism seemingly encouraged such a practice is the focus of this chapter.

How Does Racism Encourage Slavery?

There are many theories on how slavery started, but according to many scholars, the practice of placing a certain group of people into slavery dates back well into antiquity. However, one of the factors for determining whether a certain group of people can be made into slaves is race.

The notion of "inferior" races fuels the practice of slavery and usually serves to be its justification. The idea that some cultures are inferior made it "morally" sound to own others as slaves, as it would be "their place" as subservient to superior societies.

However, when we look into the violent history of human civilizations, we will realize that there are different ethnic communities whose identities have been erased through colonization. When powerful countries conducted expeditions in different parts of the world, they did so in the manner that they could own whatever land that they discovered, conquer it in the name of their kingdoms, and then claim all captured inhabitants as their slaves.

The process of colonization is an interesting thing to note when it comes to studying how racism has been ingrained as an ideology, particularly when the practice of acquiring slaves is taken into account. Since colonization involves segregation of the differing folk, and the "othering" of individuals that do not share the same identities, slavery becomes possible as a result of racism.

When colonizers adopt a racist attitude towards the inhabitants of lands that they want to conquer, they automatically hold the belief that any other people hold a much lower status than they have, regardless of their skill, knowledge, or experience. This sense of privilege and status found in most countries that have colonized other territories exist mostly because of their economic and military power, which enables them to treat others without regard to rights or civil liberties.

Now think for a second the way many humans treat dogs. It is not so much of a conscious behavior to put a dog on a leash because many pet owners view them as an animal that is able to be tamed and obey the rules of the "owner". This is the similar mindset that people took back in those days with people of another race. Since slavery, as a practice, inherently removes all rights of the slave, the life and fate of an enslaved individual is dependent on the whims of the slaver.

If you considered another race as more like an animal that is inferior, you may oftentimes also assume that their intelligence is not up to par with your own. Again, much like the religious concept, this is not to slight pet owners for owning dogs, but rather it is to just shine a light on the type of thinking that we can relate to. Sometimes people in our world today are unable to draw parallels to the people of the past because we have such trouble relating to their mindsets.

In Ancient Rome, defeated countries automatically became slaves of the Romans. Prisoners of war were often turned into slaves, especially those from Germanic, Gallic, and Carthaginian tribes. As these countries were already labeled as "barbarians", treating them no less than animals was considered acceptable.

During those times, people that were considered savages or uncivilized were subjected to utter disregard towards their identities and rights, to the point that little to none of their cultural heritage remains today.

During the rise of the Holy Roman Empire, slavery was encouraged as different ethnic groups were considered heathens, which made them humans without any existing worth. While the latter part of the Bible discourages slavery as a practice, slavery still became a practice within most Catholic countries due to certain old practices that were supported in the earlier books of the Holy Bible.

This mentality was carried over during The Dark Ages, after the decline of the Roman Empire. Slavery created the "class system", which placed people in different "tiers" of society. The upper class was considered the elite, while the peasantry was where commoners lived, and even below this, were the discriminated slaves.

It is also worth taking note that the people that were valued as slaves were those capable of work, which also leads to understanding why African slavery was more predominant in the Americas.

The reason is simpler than expected – while the early British occupants of America established slavery over the American Indians and the white servants that they had brought into the New World, they were not able to achieve the efficiency that they wanted over these races. The American Indians, for example, were far more knowledgeable than the British colonizers that colonized them, in regards to the land they lived on.

How Do Economic Necessities Produce Slavery?

As slavery was, in part, fueled by racism, slavery was also fueled by many other factors, the most influential being the economy. The economic potential of using slave labor is very profitable and most slave owning countries enjoyed an increased economic surge by taking up the practice.

Historically, slavery was reinforced by treating another race as machinery without any right for a wage. In fact, slavery was instrumental in creating monopolies ran by superpower countries, which provided economic power imbalance in their favor.

For example, the United States' cotton monopoly was created through retention of the slavery policy in the 1800s, wherein one-fifth of the nation's population was made up of African-American slaves that were toiling for little to no return. Would America have been able to attain its power without having to resolve to oppression? Many political scientists and historians do not think so.

Just think if you owned a restaurant and you didn't have to pay your worker anything but you got the same production. This is the type of thinking that many slave owners had. Human labor is pretty much the most productive labor there is. Even robots are not going to use the type of emotional intelligence a human being is capable of. This was a huge draw to the slave owners of those days.

During the late eighteenth and early nineteenth centuries, the United States grew rapidly and its economy, especially in Southern states, grew exponentially due to slave labor. The income generating potential of owning slaves is what perpetuated the practice in countries like the United States and the United Kingdom during those centuries.

Looking back to these centuries, the cotton monopoly that was created, thanks to slavery, made it possible for the United States to also exponentially expand the nation's size and economic power, which made the country capable of waging war against the British Empire and claim its independence.

However, this rise to power also led to millions of Africans being forcefully brought to the Americas to work as slaves. Most of these individuals were abducted against their own will, brought in chains, and sold in slave bazaars alongside ordinary merchandise. This is the main reason for the proliferation of African-American communities in the United States.

How Does Slavery Induce Racism?

As black slaves began to increase in number, American slave owners became more and more concerned of slave uprisings.

An example was Nat Turner, a Black preacher who rallied fellow slaves to rise up against their owners in 1831. He led a violent uprising in Southampton, Virginia, which caused the death of 55 white people. He then started to terrorize the town in a killing spree that targeted men, women, and children. The Uprising was brutally crushed by the local militia after 2 days of murder. Turner was captured a few days after the uprising and was hanged later that year.

His murderous rampage was so deeply engraved in the memory of the people in Virginia that concessions were made to drastically limit slave activity and tightened the grip on slavery even further. Turner's actions became the personification of the "black slave", which often portrayed as a savage, ignorant individual bent on misdemeanor and murder. The start of racial discrimination began to crescendo at this point, as if it hadn't been bad enough.

The impact slavery has had on the development of racial discrimination is very clear. Slavery, especially in the United States, deeply instilled racist sentiments in many "white" slave owners. This, in turn, created an environment hostile to black people, which was drastically changed in the 1960s and beyond.

Chapter 3:

Social Impact of Racism

The impact of racism in societies is very large. Cultural boundaries are often defined not only by physical borders but by racial divisions. Countless stories of alienation, neglect, and violence due to racism have stained humanity for centuries.

As different countries are now interconnected by transportation and communication, the world has indeed become smaller. This makes it possible for different cultures to intermingle, and thus also increases opportunities for racial discrimination, as well as breaking the borders of discrimination at the same time.

Inequality

The first major result of racism or racial discrimination is inequality. This was practiced many years ago by various European countries, especially the United Kingdom and the United States during the late eighteenth and most of the nineteenth centuries. However, it was only in the United States that the effect of racial oppression and slavery was so profound that it was the catalyst for the American Civil War.

As an example, during the American Civil War, black soldiers who were then called "colored" soldiers, on both Union and Confederate sides received less compensation compared to white soldiers. This was taken further by the Confederates, by limiting "Negro soldiers" to manual labor and never placing them in actual combat.

After the civil war, the abolishment of slavery came into effect, but the inequality caused by racial discrimination continued. Signs in public places reading "For Whites Only" were a rampant slogan of prejudice during the early part of the twentieth century. The level of social inequality received by African-Americans was so great that countless pleas for civil rights were made by anti-racism groups. However, the fruition of their pleas came only after the famous speech of Dr. Martin Luther King, who told America his "Dream" for the future.

The Spanish treatment of Native Americans in South America was kind, compared to the treatment of slaves in North America. Spanish "Peninsulares" – (people native of Spain) intermingled freely with Native Americans and condoned relationship and marriage, which was extremely distasteful in other countries.

In modern times, long after the social segregation in the United States ended, inequality became covert – while it had been deemed unethical and even illegal to have racial aversions in this country, many still report racial discrimination in many walks of life.

For example, the Baltimore police have been reported to target African-American residents at a higher clip than any other ethnic group in the city and county. Judicial systems in some areas also tend to fast track cases against suspects of African-American   descent.

Inefficiency

Because only part of the community is given freedom to enjoy the full benefit of being part of a society, inefficiency is the most common negative impact racist societies experience. For example, when a group of people are denied rights for education, that group will be inefficient and will become liabilities to the development of the society. On the flip side, when a society has an extremely educated population, the sky is the limit for how well the country can develop and innovate.

The lack of access to education and employment does not only impair how well one can live a dignified life, but it also creates a tremendous economic impact to a nation that serves as a melting pot of different ethnic and racial groups. America, for example, suffers a huge economic setback because of the lack of employment available to people of color, which makes up 30% of the nation's population.

Moral Degradation

One of the major results of racism is moral decay or degradation. Whenever a group of people are repressed because they are deemed inferior, it will create discontent, anger, and hate.

Among the effects of racism is othering, which is the referral to other groups or individuals as beings that do not belong. When othering happens, one forgets that another human being is made up of motivations, objectives, emotions, and ideals. That means that when a person becomes an object of racism, he/she becomes less worthy of dignity, meaning they are treated as less human and worthy of no respect.

When this happens, people that are being racist tend to forget that people that do not belong to the same culture that they have still have their own identities, which makes these people to be subject to cruelty of those that believe they have superiority.

In the United States, the *"Ku Klux Klan"* emerged as a racist group that aimed to ensure "white supremacy" in America. Because of the lack of racial empathy towards African Americans, large incidents of brutality, murder, and terrorism were inflicted towards the black community, especially in various southern states.

In Germany, during World War II, Nazism focused on upholding the belief of the superiority of the German race by attempting to suppress the proliferation of various "inferior" cultures that were present in Germany and the surrounding areas. As a result, thousands upon thousands of people were evicted from their homes, imprisoned, deported, and killed just because they were included in groups deemed "inferior" by Nazi beliefs.

This trend of racial discrimination ultimately led to the "final solution" implemented by Nazi Germany on "undesirables", namely jews, gypsies, homosexuals, various "undesired" religions, cults, and such.

Social Injustice

As racism dictates that preferences are denied to groups of people that are the focus of racist activities, injustices have serious consequences. There are many instances in recorded history that justice was denied to people because of their racial background.

In 1857, an African American slave, named Dred Scott, filed a petition to the U.S. Supreme Court to grant him his freedom on the basis of what was indicated in the Bill of Rights. However, his petition was denied. The court's reasoning was that African-Americans were not included in the Bill of Rights, as they were slaves. It was only after the signing of the Emancipation Law during the Civil War that this ruling was overturned.

This type of injustice is the result of the inculcation of racist ideas in people. Though this is one example of social injustice suffered by discriminated people, millions of unheard injustices were committed, which vanished quietly in history.

Violence

One of the inevitable outcomes of racial discrimination is violence. Aside from violence inflicted by those who are discriminating others, the retaliation of the oppressed can be more aggressive and brutal. In the history of the United States, there are many accounts of slave revolts that spread violence and terror. However, one of the most notable revolts caused by racial discrimination and slavery is the great Haitian revolt.

In 1791, discontented and oppressed Haitian slaves took arms under the leadership of General Toussaint L'Ouverture, a Haitian native, in a war for independence from France. The Haitian revolt was successful and the Republic of Haiti was born.

However, in 1794, after Haiti defeated the French forces, the British decided to reclaim the country because of its enormous economic potential. With impressive skill, the Haitian army managed to defeat the British and repulsed the invasion.

As Haiti became an independent nation, the British Empire, in retaliation for their defeat, exacted exorbitant sums of money for reparation. This pushed the country into poverty and its economic power reduced considerably. It is a twist in irony, the Haitians gained independence from a lenient France only to suffer more under the economic stranglehold of the British Empire.

Chapter 4:

Overcoming Racism

Overcoming racism is a huge task, especially nowadays. Though the level of racism is not that prevalent compared to the eighteenth and nineteenth centuries, the effects of such behavior are still seen today.

Let's delve into ways to overcome racism and how to implement change without becoming aggressive and violent.

Education

Being educated is the primary thing one can do in order to overcome racism. Remember that racism is the belief of the "superiority" of one's race and the "inferiority" of others. Education gives people the ability to "fight back" not with violence, but with intelligence. People who feel that they are being discriminated against must fight back by developing a good education and providing valuable insights.

Apart from granting access to people that are subjected to racism, it is also important for those that are enjoying a privilege to get the education that they need to understand what makes their certain actions racist or supportive of racism.

This means that by providing supposedly superior groups with the appropriate knowledge, the group will be able to understand how a huge part of society still supports segregation or the othering of other races, simply because they have a different origin or culture. When more people are able to recognize that they have actions or thoughts that put others on the sidelines or in peril, they can help people make better decisions about treating others and celebrating diversity with them.

Achievements

The illusion of superiority is the driving force for racism. In order to dissolve this illusion, one must endeavor to excel and achieve great things in life. Remember that no matter what race, nation, or country one is from, once he or she has achieved something extremely important, those lines of discrimination will be forcibly erased.

During World War II, African American pilots were considered a liability to the United States Air Force because it was believed that black people were physically and mentally unfit to handle a complicated machine such as an airplane.

This "myth" of black mediocrity was destroyed by a group of brave individuals called the "Tuskegee Airmen". This group of African-American pilots not only displayed courage during combat, but the group was among the first squadrons to enter Berlin and shoot down German Jets. This group of airmen entered into aviation legend and are now considered a group of American heroes that served during World War   II.

Understanding

In most cases, misunderstanding of various cultures is the reason for racial discrimination. It is important to create avenues of cultural exchange in order to understand other people. Without understanding, one will not be able to overcome racism.

It is important to know all about different cultures, how they developed and how similar they are to one's community. Remember that people are usually only divided by borders, language, and physical appearance, but beneath those, humanity is still a single species.

Most of the time, racial discrimination comes out of ignorance of the culture and history of other nationalities. By learning the history, culture, and traditions of other societies, one can learn to easily accept them without developing any form of prejudice. This is why educating people with the right information about other societies is extremely important.

Empathy

Respecting other people because they are human beings is the ultimate way to overcome racism. Though empathy may be induced by religion or personal beliefs, the sheer respect of other people is the best way to overcome differences and dissolve discrimination.

It is important to always have empathy towards fellow humans, as empathy strengthens the bond of people in order to cooperate and achieve large goals.

Chapter 5:

Importance of Eliminating Racism

The effects of racial discrimination are stains in the fabric of history. Racism has had a profound effect on the mentality of people and how they regard the rights of others. Because of this, many are constantly tearing the wall of racial discrimination in order to create harmony between cultures. However, why is the free interaction between cultures and equal treatment of every person that important?

Racism is a huge global problem because it hinders individualism – when people perceive that diversity should not be allowed, the potential for progress is prevented.

When you look at the bigger picture of how racism damages a large portion of the world's population, you will notice how many members of supposedly inferior races and social classes experience restricted access to opportunities, without regard that there are members of these oppressed communities that can actually provide solutions to the different world problems.

Since racism does not tolerate granting access to equal opportunities to people that belong to another race or social class, you can imagine how many people were driven from their homes or lost their lives because of racial impunity, when they could possibly become the next Lincoln or Phelps of their generation.

We can only imagine how possible positive social, economic, and political structures may collapse when discrimination is allowed to continue. Let's take a look at what the world can truly enjoy when racial discrimination ends.

Ending Racism Promotes Personal Development

By eliminating prejudices towards a particular race or group of people, it will encourage growth and development. Racism often denies people who are subjected to discrimination the means to advance and prosper. They are often pushed down the barrel and are left there to wallow in despair.

However, by ending racism, discriminated people can then gain access to necessities such as education and money, and be productive individuals who are assets to the community.

Cultural Development

By allowing different cultures a discrimination-free environment, creative contribution from everyone will be possible. This will enhance the cultural development of a society and ensure its success as it continues to grow.

The more educated a society is, the more ideas it will produce - the more ideas a society produces, the wealthier and more abundant it can become.

Happiness

The level of happiness of citizens in a country is essential to ensuring its stability. The contentment level of a country ensures that people continue to strive in order to provide value. Businesses will run smoother, productivity is ensured, and many setbacks due to unhappiness are prevented.

When racism stops, some people will stop feeling unsafe – people belonging to some minority groups will never have to feel that they need to be separated from others, or that they have limitations when it comes to taking advantages of opportunities around them.

In the future, people will never have to worry about thinking that they need to adjust to societal standards when they want to pursue happiness, since there will never be standards that people have to meet in order to attain privileges that everyone should be able to achieve.

Beneficial Contribution to Society

By allowing all people the chance to help society, their contributions can effectively push forward a community into advancement. For example, before women's suffrage, a male-dominated culture ran every aspect of society, however as women were given the chance to contribute, they drastically changed society.

This is the same when providing freedom from racial discrimination. By allowing people to contribute, their individual ideas can, in turn, help in the advancement of the society as a whole.

When the sense of privilege by the dominating classes, genders, and races are eliminated, people will finally be able to contribute to society without the risk of rejection. That also means that the rejection of privileges will lead to people being equally recognized for their contribution to the different fields of interest, enabling more people to share their skills without hindrance because of the status they are in.

Chapter 6:

Implementing A Racist-Free Environment

As racism is such a vile and inhumane practice, it is best to make sure that such behavior is removed from areas of society, such as in schools, work, businesses, and such.

Implementing a racism-free environment through personal effort is the key to accomplishing this.

Eliminating Racism in Schools

The first location to introduce the elimination of racist ideas is in school. Molding children's minds into an open acceptance of the difference in culture and appearance in people is huge for the future of the world. One can start introducing racial acceptance by including in curriculums the achievements of various cultures.

Teachers can introduce small historical snippets of famous people from all over the world; cite their achievement and how they contributed to society. By showing students the achievement made by every culture on Earth, they can see that no one is inferior, as everyone is equally capable of achieving great deeds, if given the chance.

One thing teachers or parents should stress is that people are usually a product of their environment more than any other factor out there. For example, if you were born into a single-parent, low income household, then you are more likely to be involved in criminal activity during your youth, then a person who was born into a wealthy, strong-knit family.

This is obviously not always the case, but the correlation is undeniable. It is the reason why we must strive to strengthen all families and friendships, because the more connected people feel, the better they will perform in all aspects of their life.

It is not a less-fortunate child's fault if they are struggling to find discipline in their life with all the chips stacked against them. It is the job of the communities and schools to work on bridging this gap so that when the less-fortunate children grow up, they are educated enough to break the cycle of low-opportunity.

Bullying

Though bullying is not confined to racist behavior, there are many cases where people are bullied because of racial differences. Asians, Indians, and Middle Eastern students are often the target of racial bullying.

This is especially so with people from Muslim countries because of the improper association made between Islamic traditions and terrorism.

It is very important to address incidents of bullying promptly, especially if the reasons are racial. It is vital to educate bullies to respect people as they are, and not by their race. It is also important to implement sanctions to such degrading   activity.

Simple Methods to Prevent Racial Discrimination in Classrooms

Create activities that will allow students to communicate with each other. It is important for students to know each other on a deeper level than just viewing each other as a fellow classmate. Include movies that deal with racism among the "must watch" videos in class.

Introduce anti-racism heroes and inform students of their struggles against discrimination and how they became pillars in anti-racism movements.

Eliminating Racism in the Workplace

Racism can occur in large multi-national corporations or even in the small grocery stores and shops that are just around the corner. Discrimination and racist activity at the workplace may come from a workmate, supervisor, or even from customers.

However, in order to eliminate racism, one must transform the workplace into an area that is friendly to all cultures. These are some tips on how to transform the workplace into a place where racial discrimination is minimal or non-existent:

Managers should create anti-racism policies that employees should adhere to. This set of rules should be separate from the national law and be more unique in its approach. Each company should have it's own policies that the employees work to create. By incorporating the involvement of the employees, there will be more investment from them to abide by the rules.

Instill in employees that promotions are based on skill and performance and not by racial or gender preference. If possible, conduct team building activities that will create a stronger bond between employees (especially between those of different nationalities).

Eliminating Racism in Society

Destroying racism and racial discrimination from society may be a hard thing to accomplish, but it is not impossible. The need to break patterns of racism and the cultural barrier it produces is vital in order for societies to improve and advance.

One should always remember that humankind is just a single species and everyone is connected with each other. Though people are different in many ways, these differences are only skin deep and inside each person on Earth, resides a unique individual that deserves love and respect.

People often get frustrated and feel that they have no control over racism in society. This is not true, however, because the only thing you can control is your influence in the world. You can always be a great example to others by being articulate, educated, and a productive member in society. By being an influential individual, you will begin to empower those around you to achieve great things and most importantly, you will slowly break down the barriers in society.

If you feel that someone is being racist towards you, the most productive way to handle it is to address the fact that you heard or saw the racist behavior. Stay calm and polite and don't let your emotions get in the way of relaying a message.

Remember, the reason the person or group is being racist towards you, is because they are either ignorant of your culture or they feel threatened by your success. The way to handle this is not to make them feel more threatened or scared. You must cherish the opportunity to enlighten someone and handle it with class.

After addressing the behavior, make sure to tell the person that you felt uncomfortable by the act of racism and that you would love to answer any questions that he/she may have about your race. By creating this almost awkward situation, you are forcing dialogue between you and the discriminator. Do not let the opportunity pass to encourage the person to speak his/her mind. It may be the only chance of communication this person will ever have to express something like this.

At this point, the discriminator will usually apologize. However, some will not feel bad about their discrimination and will actually give you reasons for their beliefs. While they are giving you their explanation, try your best to avoid a knee-jerk reaction or even worse, insulting them back.

Fighting discrimination with discrimination never works when dealing with racism. The best solution is to see to it that a proper dialogue occurs between the two parties involved. By being able to explain why oppression happens and why it is very important that people do not stick to discriminatory behavior, you might just be able to sway the other person to the side of peace and equality.

If possible, try to create some type of contact with this person for future reference. Explain to them that you would like to show them that judging someone negatively based on skin color or cultural background is silly. Do your best to prove that people have the same tendencies, no matter the race, it is just that we all have different opportunities which shape our behaviors.

A great way to help the person overcome their racist issues is to invite them to see your culture. This will really shock most people who are racist. They will be forced to either learn more or to publicly accept that they are choosing to remain ignorant.

You may also realize that racism is born out of a culture that is intolerant of things that exist outside the person's common education, and by inviting people who enjoy the privilege to see the world outside their comfort zones, they will understand how problematic a discriminatory worldview really is.

Now with all the guidelines for how to handle a situation involving racism, you may be thinking, why should I have to do so much just to get equal respect?

This goes back to the fact that many people who are racist are a product of their environment as well. Maybe they had nobody close to them to teach them about acceptance. Maybe they never knew a person of your race, or maybe they had one experience which turned out to be negative.

Whatever the case, you should remember that it is not necessarily about changing that one person's perception, although that is valuable in itself. It is more about the possible impact it will have on the world. If you can help that one person, how will that affect his/her interactions with other people of your race? How will it benefit his/her children, grandchildren, social circles, etc.?

Be the best example you can be, and the rest will fall into place. You can not force another person to change, but you can hold up the mirror to their face with your kindness and influence.

Conclusion

I worked hard on creating the best guide for "overcoming racism" that I could. These are all the strategies and information that has worked for me, as well as others that I have talked to and researched.

If you stay consistent and open-minded, they will work for you as well. Be optimistic about your current situation and make small progress each day!

Hopefully you were able to learn a thing or two from this book. Good luck in your own journey!